Sweet

Sixteen

16 Reasons Why You're Amazing

Reason #1

"Day by day, what you choose, what you think and what you do is who you become."

Heraclitus

Reason #2

"Time is the wisest counselor of all."

Pericles

Reason #3

"Courage is knowing what not to fear."

Plato

Reason #4

"I count him braver who overcomes his desires than him who conquers his enemies, for the hardest victory is over the self."

Aristotle

Reason #5

"We are what we repeatedly do. Excellence then, is not an act, but a habit."

Aristotle

Reason #6

"Count each day as a separate life."

Seneca

Reason #7

"The whole life of a man is but a point in time; let us enjoy it."

Plutarch

Reason #8

"Make the best use of what's in your power and take the rest as it happens."

Epictetus

Reason #9

"I love those who can smile in trouble, who can gather strength from distress, and grow brave by reflection. 'Tis the business of little minds to shrink, but they whose heart is firm, and whose conscience approves their conduct, will pursue their principles unto death."

Leonardo da Vinci

Reason #10

"I have been impressed with the urgency of doing. Knowing is not enough; we must apply. Being willing is not enough; we must do."

Leonardo da Vinci

Reason #11

"Life is like riding a bicycle. To keep your balance, you must keep moving."

Albert Einstein

Reason #12

"Once we accept our limits, we go beyond them."

Albert Einstein

Reason #13

"We know what we are, but know not what we may be."

William Shakespeare

Reason #14

"This above all; to thine own self be true."

William Shakespeare

Reason #15

"Our greatest glory is not in never failing, but in rising every time we fall."

Confucius

Reason #16

"In the midst of chaos, there is also opportunity."

Sun Tzu

Made in the USA
Columbia, SC
14 October 2020